Grades 2 – 3

60 Writing Topics

Exploring Text Types

Maureen Hyland

- Procedure
- Narrative
- Explanation
- Report
- Exposition
- Reflection

Order Number 2-5245
ISBN 1-58324-213-9

A B C D E F 09 08 07 06 05

395 Main Street
Rowley, MA 01969
www.worldteacherspress.com

Foreword

So much of life centers around the written language. This means of communication begins to influence our lives from our earliest days. It is therefore important that in educating young people we expose them to, and encourage them to become skilled in using, the many different forms of writing that will become important to them at different stages in their lives.

60 Writing Topics Grades 2 – 3 has been designed to help teachers promote and develop many different writing skills while covering a number of different areas of the curriculum. It allows both teachers and students to examine units in science, technology, health, and social education by encouraging students to use their prior knowledge of a topic, their imagination, their personal experience, and personal opinion. These and many other learning skills are highlighted in the different writing tasks that the students are asked to complete within each of six units.

Other titles in this series include:

60 Writing Topics, Grades 4 – 5
60 Writing Topics, Grades 6 – 7

Contents

Teacher's Notes

There are ten writing tasks for each unit and each task asks the student to use a different writing skill. While you will be able to assess the student's understanding of the content of a specific unit of study, these writing tasks will, most importantly, allow you to evaluate the student's understanding of, and ability to use, many different forms of writing. As the writing and reading skills of children in the elementary grades develop, they are able to move beyond the simple narrative and reflection text. Throughout the course of these units they will be able to undertake simple tasks involving the genres of procedure, report, exposition, and to a lesser extent, explanation.

Each page contains two writing tasks on a particular topic. An icon indicates the unit of work each task belongs to. The icons are relevant to the following units:

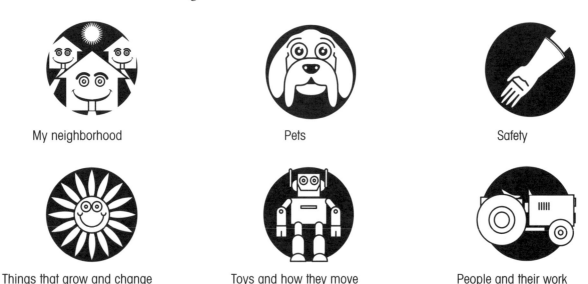

My neighborhood	Pets	Safety
Things that grow and change	Toys and how they move	People and their work

The writing topics can be copied onto colored or plain card and laminated for protection. They can be placed in a central location for students to access easily. You may assign the tasks or the students may choose their own.

A student checklist has been provided for the students to record the topics used. A teacher checklist has also been included so that you can monitor the progress of the class and to ensure that all students are practicing each writing genre. This may be enlarged to display in the room. Students should choose topics which cover a variety of writing genres. Should you wish to assign a writing task as a group activity, multiple copies may be made. You may find these invaluable during group language sessions.

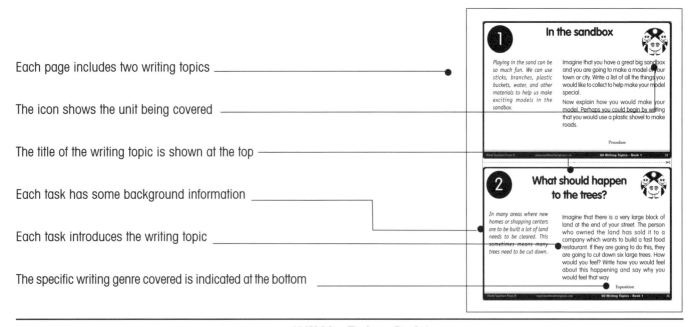

Each page includes two writing topics

The icon shows the unit being covered

The title of the writing topic is shown at the top

Each task has some background information

Each task introduces the writing topic

The specific writing genre covered is indicated at the bottom

Teacher's Notes

What to Look for When Assessing a Student's Understanding of a Particular Genre

The following information provides you with a definition of each of the writing genres, an outline of the structure of the texts, and some of the specific language features, that when used, show an understanding of the genre in question. Not all of the language features will be evident in the texts of elementary students, but this outline will enable you to monitor the progress of the students as their writing skills develop.

Narrative

Definition of a narrative: A narrative is a text that tells a story. Narratives are generally imaginative but can be based on factual information. Narratives can take on a variety of forms such as short stories, myths, poems, and fairytales.

Text structure: A narrative consists of three parts:

(a) an introduction, where the setting is presented, characters introduced, and time set for the event/s to occur.

(b) a complication or conflict, where problems arise concerning the main character(s).

(c) a resolution or conclusion where the problems of the character/s are resolved.

Special language features: use of words that link stages in time, descriptive enhancement by use of adjectives and adverbs, use of action verbs to highlight physical and mental processes and can be written in first or third person.

Reflection

Definition of a reflection: A reflection is a text that tells about past experiences or events. They can be based on the author's personal experience, on historical events, or it can be imaginative, whereby the author has no direct link to recalled events.

Text structure: Most reflections begin with some form of orientation where the who? what? when? where? and why? of the text are introduced. This is followed by a chronologically ordered set of events. There can be some form of concluding statement or reorientation at the end.

Special language features: use of past tense, correct sequencing of events, words related to time, inclusion of action verbs, and personal comments.

Report

Definition of a report: A report is a text that consists of an organized factual record of events or a classification and description of one or many things. It can be related to the present day or be based around something from the past.

Text structure: Begins with a general statement or introduction that indicates the nature of the topic upon which the report is based. This is followed by a description of the various features relevant to the topic. In some cases this can take on the form of "named" paragraphs or subheadings. It can conclude with a summarizing statement.

Special language features: vocabulary related to specific topic, action verbs, words identifying classifications, and descriptive language.

Procedure

Definition of a procedure: A procedure explains how to make or do something.

Text structure: Most procedural texts begin with an outline of what is to be achieved, or an aim. This is followed by a list of required materials and then step by step instructions to reach the goal. The text can conclude with an evaluation.

Special language features: words of commands, words used to link stages of procedure, sequential ordering of steps, action verbs, and detailed information, for example, size, amount, weight.

Exposition

Definition of an exposition: An exposition aims to present and develop ideas in the form of a logical argument. The text can be one sided, or, it can address both sides of an argument allowing the reader to form an opinion from the information presented.

Text structure: Most expositions begin with a statement which introduces the issue that will be addressed. This is followed by arguments with evidence to support the stance. A conclusion summarizes the presentation or suggests that the reader now form an opinion.

Special language features: use of topic-related vocabulary, use of connectives to reinforce results of actions, thinking verbs used to express opinion, and the use of emotive and persuasive language.

Explanation

Definition of an explanation: An explanation is a text that outlines how or why things occur, or how things operate.

Text structure: An explanatory text begins with a statement about what is to be explained. This is followed by details of sequential events or stages in operation. It usually ends with some form of concluding statement.

Special language features: use of topic-specific vocabulary, words that outline cause and effect and words identifying time relationships, for example, following, then; and the use of present tense.

Suggestions for Use

The writing tasks included in this book are intended to be a multi-use resource for the teacher in the classroom. Therefore, the suggestions listed below are in no way definitive, but just some of the possible uses. You should choose only those activities which are appropriate to the ability levels and literacy experiences of their students.

Specific writing genre tasks

Each writing genre is explained carefully, showing a definition of the genre, the structure and special language features of the text. After students have been exposed to each specific genre, the writing topics may be used to reinforce their concept of the genre.

Student checklist of the use of specific text types

Once the students are familiar with a particular writing genre, the writing topics may be used specifically by the students to gauge their own progress. A self-assessment checklist has been included for the students to monitor their use of the structures and features of each genre. Features of text types may be found on pages 5 – 6 and also on the student checklist on page 9. The features of each text type have been included on page 9 with check boxes for the student to verify that he/she has included all the necessary features. Multiple copies will be needed.

Writing specific to a particular theme

Each of the six themes has ten writing topics relating to it. Teachers who are covering a particular theme will be able to utilize the writing topics to reinforce and add interest to the theme.

Portfolio assessment tasks

The writing tasks may be used as an assessment activity in the English learning area, after the students have been exposed to and practiced the specific writing genres. To assist you to use the writing topics in this way, a portfolio assessment form has been included. The student's writing topic activity may be stapled to the form. A checklist assists you in assessing whether the student has included the structures and features necessary for that particular genre. Other aspects of language, such as spelling and grammar, may be assessed at the same time. A sample assessment form for each text type is included on pages 10 to 17. A blank worksheet may be found on page 11.

Group/Individual language activities

The writing topics may be used during group language sessions, with specific topics or tasks given to individuals or groups. Multiple copies of a particular card may be made for group work.

Student self-assessment

Student self-assessment, using the student checklist, allows the students to monitor their progress in the use of specific writing genres. As students become more familiar with the features and structures of each writing genre, they will be able to monitor their increased use of these in each writing genre. This self-assessment format may be useful for the student to use when involved in three-way conferences among parents, you, and himself/herself. A sample form is included on page 18.

Comparison/Conversion of text types

Using the writing topics, you may compare one writing genre with another. Students can observe and use the different structures and features within their own writing. Students may be required to convert one text type into another, making sure to include the relevant structures and features. A format for comparing text types is included on page 19. A worksheet to convert one text type to another is included on page 20.

Extension/Reinforcement activities

Every classroom has students of varying abilities, talents, working habits, and personalities. Students who are fast workers may be rewarded with their choice of a writing topic to complete until the other students finish. Students who have difficulty completing a specific writing genre may be given writing topics to reinforce that particular genre, as long as they have not completed the task before.

*Creating writing topics

Using the writing topics as a guide, the students may be required to create writing topics of their own relating to a specific writing genre. These topics may be exchanged within the class, completed, and evaluated. A writing topic which many students have difficulty completing may not be suitable for the specific writing genre. A writing topic which students can easily shape to suit a specific genre is a suitable writing topic. A blank worksheet to enable students to create their own writing topics is included on page 21.

*This type of activity is only suitable for very competent or older students.

Reinforcement/Assessment of features of language/handwriting

Using the writing topic, you may be able to evaluate the student's knowledge of grammar concepts, punctuation, spelling, and handwriting. One task may be used to assess or reinforce a number of outcomes. This can be a time saving activity for you.

Planning/Reviewing/Changing text types

The planning of a writing form can be complex and daunting for students. An obvious format, with specific structures and features, allows the students the security to write personal topics within a given framework, while still allowing some flexibility.

Modeling Writing

You may use similar titles for particular themes to model the different writing genre for the students. Try to avoid using those exact titles used in the writing topics so that students are creating their own ideas when using the task cards.

Motivational Ideas

Students need motivation to encourage creative ideas. Since the writing topics are being used as an individual activity, it is difficult to inspire each student before he or she begins each writing topic. The following ideas are suggested as a reference for students to use before they begin their writing topic:

- You could provide visual displays of particular themes near the writing topics box; for example, toys brought in by the students, photographs, newspaper clippings, and posters. When displays are changed, each display can be recorded on camera and photographs and digital pictures displayed for other students to view.

- Students who finish quickly may find extra pictures in magazines to add to class books on particular themes.

- Banks of word lists for particular themes can be recorded and displayed for future reference.

- Displays of other students' work on the same topic may be viewed to encourage ideas.

- Display theme books from the library relevant to a particular writing theme.

- Provide and display outlines of the writing forms for students to refer to when writing (see pages 5 and 6).

- Where possible, allow students access to a computer to research a particular theme or writing topic.

Teacher Checklist

Use this chart to record the WRITING TOPICS that have been completed.

Student Name	My neighborhood										Pets										Safety										Things that grow and change										Toys and how they move										People and their work									
	1	2	3	4	5	6	7	8	9	10	11	12	13	14	15	16	17	18	19	20	21	22	23	24	25	26	27	28	29	30	31	32	33	34	35	36	37	38	39	40	41	42	43	44	45	46	47	48	49	50	51	52	53	54	55	56	57	58	59	60

Student Checklist

Use this chart to record the WRITING TOPICS that have been completed.

My neighborhood

1	2	3	4	5	6	7	8	9	10
In the sun box	What should happen to the trees?	Once upon a time	Time to celebrate	Postal worker for a day	Keeping it clean	Off to the mall	It's picnic time	For sale	How does the water come from the tap?

Comment

Pets

11	12	13	14	15	16	17	18	19	20
Oh! what a pet	Getting ready	Keeping a pet bird	A day in a police car	My dream pet	What do you think?	Stuck up a tree	Clever pets	Inside or outside	The pet show	A little bit frightened

Comment

Safety

21	22	23	24	25	26	27	28	29	30
The crossing guard	What was wrong?		What should I do?	Taking care with electricity	Feeling safe and happy at school	Safely at the beach	Stop the fires	Safely near the pool	Bicycle safely

Comment

Things that grow and change

31	32	33	34	35	36	37	38	39	40
The magic beanstalk	What makes me grow healthy and strong?	Helping the plant to grow	Tiny, tiny little thing	What you think of grandparents	Special things I remember	The changing tree	Dyed hair	Old for a day	A clever bird

Comment

Toys and how they move

41	42	43	44	45	46	47	48	49	50
How does it work?	The magic hobby-horse	My very own toy	Memories	Can it be dangerous?	In the toy shop	It's for sale	A broken toy	I was so scared	My favorite toy

Comment

People and their work

51	52	53	54	55	56	57	58	59	60
Police at work	What did my teacher do?	An important job	What will I be?	Computer teacher	From the cow to the shop	A farmer's magical adventure	Work, work, work	Getting paid	The school custodian

Comment

Student Text Type Checklist

Name _____ Date _____

Narrative

1. Introduces the setting, time and character(s). ☐

2. Includes a sequence of events involving the main character(s). ☐

3. Includes a complication or conflict involving the main character(s). ☐

4. Includes a resolution to the complication or a conclusion. ☐

5. Uses a range of conjunctions to connect ideas. ☐

6. Writes in meaningful paragraphs. ☐

7. Uses descriptive language. ☐

8. Writes in the past tense. ☐

Comment _____
_____
_____
_____

Reflection

1. Introduces all relevant background in a clearly written orientation (who, when, where, why). ☐

2. Includes significant events in detail. ☐

3. Includes significant events in chronological order. ☐

4. Uses vocabulary to suggest time passing. ☐

5. Writes in paragraphs to show separate sections. ☐

6. Maintains the past tense. ☐

7. Writes a conclusion with an evaluative comment. ☐

Comment _____
_____
_____
_____

Report

1. Begins with a general or classifying statement. ☐

2. Includes accurate, detailed descriptions. ☐

3. Uses factual rather than imaginative language. ☐

4. Writes in the third person. ☐

5. Writes in the present tense. ☐

6. Uses linking and action verbs. ☐

Comment _____
_____
_____
_____

Procedure

1. States the purpose of the procedure clearly and precisely. ☐

2. Lists the materials or requirements under appropriate headings or layout. ☐

3. Presents the method in a detailed, logical sequence. ☐

4. Begins instructions with an imperative verb. ☐

5. Uses subject-specific vocabulary. ☐

6. Writes in simple present tense. ☐

7. Includes an evaluation (if appropriate). ☐

Comment _____
_____
_____

Exposition

1. Begins with an opening statement presenting a general view of the topic. ☐

2. Presents "for" and "against" arguments in a logical manner. ☐

3. Uses supporting details in presenting each argument. ☐

4. Uses an impersonal style of writing. ☐

5. Uses a variety of controlling words and conjunctions. ☐

6. Uses paragraphs to state and elaborate on each point. ☐

7. Writes an evaluative conclusion.

Comment _____
_____
_____

Explanation

1. Begins with a precise statement or definition. ☐

2. Includes subject-specific terms and technical vocabulary where appropriate. ☐

3. Gives a clear account in logical sequence of how and why the phenomenon occurs. ☐

4. Uses simple present tense. ☐

5. Uses linking words to show cause and effect. ☐

6. Includes an evaluation (if necessary). ☐

Comment _____
_____
_____

60 Writing Topics – Book 1

Portfolio Assessment

Name _____ Date _____

Glue student writing task here.
(Staple student writing to the back.)

(TASK) The student was asked to write a _____ including all structures and features of the text type.

English		Writing	
Indicators		Demonstrated	Needs Further Opportunity
• Writes a _____.		☐	☐
• Includes all structures and features.		☐	☐

Teacher Comment _____

_____

_____

_____

_____

Portfolio Assessment – Narrative

Name _____ Date _____

Glue student writing task here.
(Staple student writing to the back.)

TASK The student was asked to write a narrative including all structures and features of the text type.

Indicators	Demonstrated	Needs Further Opportunity
• Writes a narrative.	☐	☐
• Includes all structures and features.		
1. *Introduces the setting, time, and character(s).*	☐	☐
2. *Includes a sequence of events involving the main character(s).*	☐	☐
3. *Includes a complication or conflict involving the main character(s).*	☐	☐
4. *Includes a resolution or conclusion to the complication.*	☐	☐
5. *Uses a range of conjunctions to connect ideas.*	☐	☐
6. *Writes in meaningful paragraphs.*	☐	☐
7. *Uses descriptive language.*	☐	☐
8. *Writes in the past tense.*	☐	☐

Teacher Comment _____

_____

_____

Portfolio Assessment – Reflection

Name _____ Date _____

Glue student writing task here.
(Staple student writing to the back.)

TASK The student was asked to write a reflection including all structures and features of the text type.

Indicators	Demonstrated	Needs Further Opportunity
• Writes a reflection.	☐	☐
• Includes all structures and features.		
1. Introduces all relevant background in a clearly written orientation (who, when, where, why).	☐	☐
2. Includes significant events in detail.	☐	☐
3. Includes significant events in chronological order.	☐	☐
4. Uses vocabulary to suggest time passing.	☐	☐
5. Writes in paragraphs to show separate sections.	☐	☐
6. Maintains the past tense.	☐	☐
7. Writes a conclusion with an evaluative comment	☐	☐

Teacher Comment _____

_____

_____

Portfolio Assessment – Report

Name _____ Date _____

Glue student writing task here.
(Staple student writing to the back.)

TASK The student was asked to write a report including all structures and features of the text type.

Indicators	Demonstrated	Needs Further Opportunity
• Writes a report.	☐	☐
• Includes all structures and features.		
1. *Begins with a general or classifying statement.*	☐	☐
2. *Includes accurate detailed descriptions.*	☐	☐
3. *Uses factual language rather than imaginative.*	☐	☐
4. *Writes in the third person.*	☐	☐
5. *Writes in the present tense.*	☐	☐
6. *Uses linking and action verbs.*	☐	☐

Teacher Comment _____

_____

_____

_____

Portfolio Assessment – Procedure

Name _____ Date _____

Glue student writing task here.
(Staple student writing to the back.)

 TASK The student was asked to write a procedure including all structures and features of the text type.

Indicators

	Demonstrated	Needs Further Opportunity
• Writes a procedure.	☐	☐
• Includes all structures and features.		
1. States the purpose of the procedure clearly and precisely.	☐	☐
2. Lists the materials or requirements under appropriate headings or layout.	☐	☐
3. Presents the method in a detailed, logical sequence.	☐	☐
4. Begins instructions with an imperative verb.	☐	☐
5. Uses subject-specific vocabulary.	☐	☐
6. Writes in a simple present tense.	☐	☐
7. Includes an evaluation (if appropriate).	☐	☐

Teacher Comment _____

_____

_____

Portfolio Assessment – Exposition

Name _____ Date _____

Glue student writing task here.
(Staple student writing to the back.)

TASK The student was asked to write an exposition including all structures and features of the text type.

Indicators	Demonstrated	Needs Further Opportunity
• Writes an exposition.	☐	☐
• Includes all structures and features.		
1. *Begins with an opening statement presenting a general view of the subject.*	☐	☐
2. *Presents "for" and "against" arguments in a logical manner.*	☐	☐
3. *Uses supporting details in presenting each argument.*	☐	☐
4. *Uses an impersonal style of writing.*	☐	☐
5. *Uses a variety of controlling words and conjunctions.*	☐	☐
6. *Uses paragraphs to state and elaborate on each point.*	☐	☐
7. *Writes an evaluative conclusion.*	☐	☐

Teacher Comment _____

_____

_____

Portfolio Assessment – Explanation

Name _____ Date _____

Glue student writing task here.
(Staple student writing to the back.)

TASK The student was asked to write an explanation including all structures and features of the text type.

Indicators	Demonstrated	Needs Further Opportunity
• Writes an explanation.	☐	☐
• Includes all structures and features.		
1. *Begins with a precise statement or definition.*	☐	☐
2. *Includes subject-specific terms and technical vocabulary.*	☐	☐
3. *Gives a clear account in logical sequence of how and why the phenomenon occurs.*	☐	☐
4. *Uses simple present tense.*	☐	☐
5. *Uses linking words to show cause and effect.*	☐	☐
6. *Includes an evaluation (if necessary).*	☐	☐

Teacher Comment _____

_____

_____

_____

Student Self-Assessment

Name _____ Date _____

Glue student writing task here.
(Staple student writing to the back.)

Text Type _____

Features of text	Student Self-Assessment	Features of text	Student Self-Assessment
• _____	☺	• _____	☺
• _____	☺	• _____	☺
• _____	☺	• _____	☺
• _____	☺	• _____	☺

In my next _____, I will need to _____

_____

Comparison of Text Types

Name _____ Date _____

Text Type 1 _____

Text Type 2 _____

Similar Features

_____

_____

_____

Different Features

_____

_____

_____

Text type [ ] has the most features.

Text type [ ] has the least features.

Text type [ ] is easier to write.

Text type [ ] is harder to write.

Conversion of Text Types

Name _____ Date _____

Glue student writing task here.
(Staple extra student writing to the back.)

In the space below, rewrite your writing topic using a different text type. Try to include all the features of the new text type.

I have chosen to convert my writing task to a _____.

_____

_____

_____

_____

Creating Writing Topics

Use the same format below to create your own writing topic.

Don't forget to include:

- a title for your writing topic
- a theme (you may draw the icon to match)
- a number for your topic
- an introduction to the topic
- the writing task
- the text type required

Ask a friend to complete your writing task.

Wrapped in Writing

Name _____ Date _____

Signed _____

Writing Wiz

Name _____

Date _____

Signed _____

Wicked Writing

Name _____

Date _____

Signed _____

Wriggling Through Writing

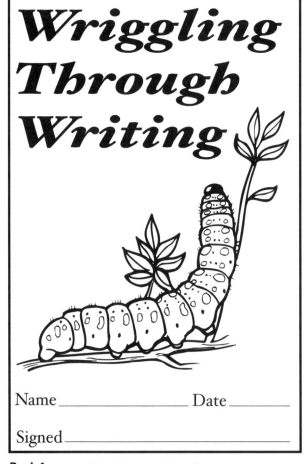

Name _____ Date _____

Signed _____

1 In the sandbox

Playing in the sand can be so much fun. We can use sticks, branches, plastic buckets, water, and other materials to help us make exciting models in the sandbox.

Imagine that you have a great big sandbox and you are going to make a model of your town or city. Write a list of all the things you would like to collect to help make your model special.

Now explain how you would make your model. Perhaps you could begin by writing that you would use a plastic shovel to make roads.

Procedure

2 What should happen to the trees?

In many areas where new homes or shopping centers are to be built a lot of land needs to be cleared. This sometimes means many trees need to be cut down.

Imagine that there is a very large block of land at the end of your street. The person who owned the land has sold it to a company which wants to build a fast food restaurant. If they are going to do this, they are going to cut down six large trees. How would you feel? Write how you would feel about this happening and say why you would feel that way.

Exposition

3 Once upon a time

Once upon a time, three bears went to visit a house in their neighborhood. It was Goldilocks's house and what mischief they got up to! Let's pretend that it's lunchtime at school. While you and your friends have been outside playing, there have been some visitors in your classroom!

Write your own story about the visitors. What kind of creatures were they? How many were there? What mischief did they get up to? If you like, you can begin your story with "Once upon a time."

Narrative

---

4 Time to celebrate

At some time during each year most towns, cities, and villages have a special celebration of their own. It might be a fair, a festival, a concert, or a circus.

Write about a special celebration that you attended in your neighborhood. Write about the type of celebration, where it was held, who went, and how much you enjoyed it.

Reflection

Postal worker for a day

Every day from Monday to Saturday, the post office delivers letters and packages around your area. Imagine that last week you were asked to be the person delivering the mail for just one day. What an experience!

You are resting your feet at the end of your busy day. Write about your experiences as the postal worker. Explain where you went and what you saw. Also include something about the most exciting and most difficult part of your day.

Reflection

Keeping it clean

Most people keep their homes and gardens very tidy. Sometimes, however, people drop rubbish in the streets and don't bother to clean it up. They think that someone else will come along and do it.

Do you think that it is all right for people to drop their rubbish out in the street, or do you think that everyone should help to keep your town or city clean? Think about this question. Write as many points as possible to show why you think the way you do.

Exposition

Off to the mall

7

You might live a long way from the mall or you might be very close to some. Think about some of the things that you walk or drive past on the way to the nearest mall. These might be an old building or some traffic lights. Perhaps there's a farm or a swimming pool.

Draw lines to divide your page into six sections. In each section draw a picture of something that you pass on the way to the mall. You must draw your pictures in order, so the first picture will be of something not far from your house. Write a sentence explaining each picture.

Procedure

It's picnic time

8

Picnics can be great fun. We can have a picnic in a park, at the beach, near a river, or even in our own backyard. Some picnics can be very adventurous. It's time to write your own adventure story.

Pretend that you and some friends go on a picnic not very far from your home. While you are on your picnic something really amazing happens. Write a story telling everything that happens during that adventure.

Narrative

9 For sale

When a house or building is for sale a real estate agent usually puts an advertisement in the paper that tells people all the special things about the building. The sign might say that the house has three bedrooms, a big family room, a swimming pool, two garages, and a beautiful garden.

Pretend that your house is for sale. Write an advertment that tells about all the special features of your home. Draw a picture of your home first.

Report

---

10 How does the water come from the tap?

If you live in the country, you might have a big water tank in your backyard. If you live on a farm you may have a dam. In the city, your water might come from a very big water reservoir. Wherever we live, most of us are lucky enough to be able to turn on a tap and have a drink of water when we are thirsty.

How does the water get into the tap? Write about how you think we are able to turn on a tap and watch water run out. Where does it come from? How does it get all the way to the tap?

Explanation

Oh! What a pet

Families can own a variety of pets. Some pets can be very large, like a horse. Others can be small, like a goldfish or lizard. It's time for you to invent the most amazing pet ever.

Write a story about an imaginary pet. As you write about the adventures the two of you have, don't forget to give your pet a name, describe what it looks like, and list what it eats.

Narrative

Getting ready

If someone at home told you that you were going to get a new dog, there are many things that you would need to do. You have to prepare very carefully for any new pet.

Think about the new dog and how big it is going to grow. Write about all the things you would have to do before you could bring the puppy home. Try to write all the information in the order you would do it. Perhaps the first thing would be to build it a kennel.

Procedure

Keeping a pet bird

13

When we write a report about anything we only include things that are true. That means we can't just make it up. Think about a pet bird. There are many important facts that we need to know if we are going to keep one of these creatures at home.

Write a report about keeping a pet bird. You could begin by saying that all pets need to be cared for. You can then write as many facts as you know. Include what a bird can be kept in, what it needs to eat and drink, how it can be kept clean, and if it needs to be protected from anything.

Report

My dream pet

14

Many people have some type of pet at home. The most common pets are cats, dogs, and birds. Sometimes we see an animal in places like pet shops or at the zoo or sanctuary and we dream of having that animal as a pet.

Write about a time when you saw an animal somewhere that you thought you would love to have at home with you. Include where you saw the pet, a description of it, who you were with, and what made you feel the way you did.

Reflection

15   What do you think?

Different types of pets have different needs. Dogs need room to run around, or they need to be walked. Fish need pond weeds or some sort of food to eat. Horses have to be groomed and exercised regularly. Think about the needs of a bird.

Do you think it is all right for large birds such as cockatoos and parrots to be kept in cages? Once you have given yourself some time to think about this question, write all your thoughts on paper.

Exposition

---

16   Stuck up a tree

Cats can jump down from very high places and land on their feet, but they sometimes get too frightened. There are often stories in newspapers and on television about firefighters having to rescue cats stuck high up in a tree or on the roofs of houses.

Pretend that you work for a newspaper and you have just seen a cat get rescued by a firefighter. Write a report for your newspaper about what you saw.

Report

Clever pets

Some pets can be taught to do very clever tricks. Before they learn to do the tricks properly, their owners usually have to work very hard at teaching them.

Think about three different tricks you could teach a dog. Explain exactly what you would have to do to train the dog. This is an example—if you wanted to teach the dog to fetch a ball, what would be the first step you would take? What would you do next?

Procedure

Inside or outside

There are some people who keep their pets inside. Some dogs, cats, birds, and even fish spend most of their time inside people's homes. There are other people who never let their pets come inside.

Do you think pets should be allowed to spend a lot of time inside a home? Think about this question and then write all the reasons why you think the way you do.

Exposition

The pet show

19

Many people enter their pets in animal shows. At these shows, judges look at the size of the animals, their fur or their feathers, and sometimes the way they walk. The animals and their owners can win trophies and ribbons.

Write an imaginative story about a pet that you entered in a show. Don't forget to describe the pet, where the show was held, what you did to your pet before the show, and some special points about the judging. Finish your story by writing about how you felt after the show.

Narrative

A little bit frightened

20

Most people love their pets and enjoy spending time with them. Sometimes, if we visit other people, we can be a little bit frightened by their pets. This might be because they are big, because they are nasty, or just because we are not used to them.

Think about a time when you went to visit someone and you were frightened by their pets. It might have been a long time ago when you were very little. Write about what happened on that day.

Reflection

The crossing guard

21

Children who need to cross big roads to get to and from school will often find someone working at a crossing near their school to help them cross the road. This person might be called a crossing guard or a "lollipop person." He or she must make sure all cars have stopped before letting children step onto the road.

Write what you think about the following sentence:

All school crossings should have a crossing guard.

Exposition

✂

What was wrong?

22

Sometimes people do unsafe things. You have probably seen someone cross the road when the light was red, someone drive a car too fast, or someone swim outside the ropes at the beach. It is very dangerous to do any of these things.

Write about a time when you saw someone do something that was unsafe. Remember to say where it happened, who did it, what he or she did, and what the danger was.

Reflection

23   What should I do?

There have probably been many times when you have had to cross a busy road. Even when you have a grown-up with you there are certain things you need to do when crossing a road so that you are not in any danger.

Draw lines to divide your page into four sections. Draw four pictures to show the steps you should take when you are about to cross a road. Write a sentence under each picture, to explain what is happening.

Procedure

✂

24   A day in a police car

The police do many things to help people feel safe. They stop people doing bad things, they tell people about safety, and they are there to help us when we need them. The police do many different jobs in one day.

Write an imaginative story about spending a day working with the police. Begin by explaining why you are doing it and who will be with you. Write about all the exciting things that happen in the day, including traveling in the police car. Finish the story by saying how you felt at the end of the day.

Narrative

25 Taking care with electricity

There are many things in our homes that need electricity to make them work. Electricity is a wonderful thing. It helps us to stay warm or cool, to cook food, wash clothes, take a shower, and iron clothes. However, electricity around the home can also be very dangerous.

Write a report about how electricity can be dangerous around the home if people are not careful. Ask your teacher if you can share this important report with your classmates.

Report

---

26 Feeling safe and happy at school

When new children start at your school, it is important that they feel it is a safe and happy place to come each day. Right from when you first started school your teacher would have spoken to you about how to treat other children and how to make sure everyone feels safe.

At the top of your page write this sentence:

There are many things that I can do to make someone feel safe and happy at school.

Now, write all the things you can do. Begin with what you can do first, then the next thing you could do, and keep going until you can't think of any more points. At the very end, write how you think all this would make a new person feel.

Procedure

27 Safety at the beach

When your parents or other grown-ups took you to the beach, they would have told you about being careful. We don't only have to be careful in the water, we also need to be careful on the sand.

Think about a time when you visited the beach. Write all the things that you can remember about that day, especially all the things that you and your family or your friends did to stay safe.

Reflection

28 Stop the fires

Every year when summer approaches there are many reports on the radio and television and in the newspapers about all the things that people should do to stop forest fires and house fires. It is very important that everyone pays attention to these reports.

Pretend that you are a news reporter for your local paper. Write a report that tells the readers all the fire safety things they need to do when summer is nearly here. You might like to start your report with one of these sentences:

Everyone needs to prepare as summer approaches.

or

Fire safety is important for everyone.

Report

Safety near the pool

It is important that there are fences around swimming pools which people have in their backyards. This is for safety reasons. When we go to local swimming pools we are also asked to behave safely. There are warning signs at some big pools.

At the local swimming pool there was a sign that said:

Children must be supervised at all times.

Use a dictionary or talk to your teacher about the word "supervised." Now, write all the reasons why you agree or disagree with the message on this sign.

Exposition

Bicycle safety

It's lots of fun to go for a ride on your bicycle. There are now many bike paths that go through beautiful areas near parks, rivers, and places with many trees. If we obey safety rules we can really enjoy these bike rides.

Draw a picture of someone riding a bicycle. Underneath, write all the safety things that are important when someone is going for a ride. Don't forget to mention what they should wear, how they should ride, and what they should do if someone else is walking or riding on the same path.

Report

The magic beanstalk

Once upon a time, Jack threw some beans out of the window and they grew into a magic beanstalk. He climbed the beanstalk and had some very strange adventures at the top. He found a giant and a goose that laid golden eggs.

Write your own story about a magic beanstalk. You could be the one to plant the beans. What will you find at the top of your beanstalk? What adventures will you have?

Narrative

What makes me grow healthy and strong?

You were very little when you were born, but each year you have grown a little more. You are also a lot stronger now than when you were a baby. If you want to keep growing, and you want to stay healthy and strong, there are some important things that you need to do.

Write this sentence at the top of your page:

To grow healthy and strong, there are some important things that people should do.

Now write all the things that you know people need to do if they are going to grow up healthy and strong.

Report

33 Helping the plant to grow

People who work in plant nurseries grow many kinds of plants and trees. They need to take very good care of the plants so that people will come and buy them for their own gardens. If we grow seeds or small plants that we want to grow into trees or bushes, there are some important things we need to do.

If you went to the nursery and brought home a small plant, how would you help it to grow into a big tree? Write a list of all the garden things you would need to use and then explain all the steps you would take to help the plant grow.

Procedure

✂

34 Tiny, tiny little thing

When a baby is born, it is very tiny. Kittens, puppies, and rabbits are also very tiny when they are born. Even a huge tree begins as a tiny seed. Sometimes it is hard for us to imagine that these little things can grow to be very big things.

Think back to a time when you saw something that had hardly grown at all. It might have been a baby or an animal or a plant. Write about when you first saw it. Include where you saw it, what it was, a description of it, and how you felt when you saw it.

Reflection

35

What do you think of grandparents?

Some people are young and some people are older. Some people have grey hair and some people do not have very much hair at all. I wonder when people start to feel old.

Think about this sentence:

Grandparents are old.

Do you think this is true? Write all the things that this sentence makes you think about. While you are doing this you might like to think about your own grandparents or the grandparents of one of your friends.

Exposition

36

Special things I remember

There are some special things in our lives that we never forget. Already you will be able to remember some very important things that you don't want to forget. These might include starting school, a special birthday or a new baby brother or sister being born.

Draw lines to divide your page into four boxes. In each box draw a picture of something special you can remember from a long time ago. Draw your pictures in order. Underneath each, write how old you were and what you can remember about the event.

Reflection

The changing tree

Wouldn't it be funny if our hair changed color every time it was autumn and by the time winter came we had no hair at all? Maybe, then in the springtime new hair would grow. If we were trees, this would happen. There are some trees, like fruit trees, which change with the seasons.

Draw lines to divide your page into four sections. At the top of each section write one of the seasons—summer, autumn, winter, or spring. In each of the squares draw a picture of what a fruit tree might look like during that season. Underneath each picture write a sentence about what happens to the tree in that season.

Report

38

Dyed hair

Do you still have the same color hair that you had when you were born? Often, as people get older the color of their hair will change. Some people who are born with dark hair can have fair hair by the time they are ten years old. Sometimes people change the color of their hair by using special dye.

Do you think elementary school children should be allowed to dye their hair? Write what you think about this question.

Exposition

Old for a day

Sometimes we can look at people and wonder what they do all day. You know a lot about what children your age do, but what does a very old person do all day?

It's imagination time! Imagine that you are a very old person for just one day. Write a story about all that you do during the day. Begin by saying who you are, where you are, and what you are about to do. Share all your adventures for that day.

Narrative

A clever bird

When a female bird grows and is about to become a mother, she has to build something special in which she can lay her eggs. She needs a place that will be safe for the eggs and warm for the baby birds.

What would be the first thing the bird would have to do when it was going to build a nest? Once you have thought about this, explain how you think the bird would go about building the nest, from the beginning until it was completed.

Explanation

41 — How does it work?

Toys move in many different ways. Some spin, some roll, and others go up and down. Some toys need batteries to make them move, some need to be pushed, and others use springs or levers.

Think of a moving toy you own or one that belongs to a friend. Draw a picture of the toy. Underneath the picture, explain how the toy moves. Include what you have to do to the toy before it will begin to move.

Explanation

✂

42 — The magic hobbyhorse

A hobbyhorse is an interesting toy. Most of these have a plastic or a wooden horse head that sits on the end of a pole. Some hobbyhorses have wheels at the bottom of the pole.

Imagine that you were given a hobbyhorse as a birthday present. Today is the first chance you've had to ride it and something magical is about to happen. You won't need to use your feet because the horse will suddenly begin to move all by itself. Write about your adventures.

Narrative

43 My very own toy

We can use some simple materials such as blocks of wood, lids from jam jars, nails, cardboard, and split pins to make toys that move. Think about a moving toy that you could make.

Begin by listing all the things that you will need to make your toy, such as a hammer, nails, a block of wood, and so on. Now write exactly how you will go about making your toy. Number each of the things you would do in order, from the first thing to the very last thing. (The last thing might be to paint your toy.)

Procedure

---

44 Memories

We usually receive some type of gift for our birthday. There are special people in our lives who always remember these occasions. Try to think of a toy that can move that you were given as a present. It might be a car, a doll, a yoyo, or a spinning top.

Use a piece of cardboard to make a "thank you" card for the person who gave you the toy. You could draw a picture of the toy on the cover. Inside, write a letter to tell the person how you felt when you opened the present.

Reflection

45 Can it be dangerous?

Some simple toys can have very small parts, such as car wheels, doll's eyes, and little springs. Most children your age know how to play carefully with toys, but very little children often think that everything can be eaten.

Do you think parents should buy toys that contain small parts for their little children?

Write down how you feel about this question. See how many different reasons you can give for feeling the way you do.

Exposition

46 In the toy store

You have probably spent a lot of time looking at toys in toy stores. There are always so many different things to see. There must be people inventing new toys all the time. How exciting it would be to live in a toy store.

Write a story about a toy that comes to life in the store. Describe the toy and write all about what it does when it comes to life.

Narrative

It's for sale

When shops have big sales they often get people to put little booklets or catalogs into mailboxes. These catalogs can be great to look at, especially if they're from a toy store. Let's see if we can sell a special toy.

On a large sheet of paper draw a picture of a toy that can move in some way. At the top of the picture write the name of the toy. Underneath the picture write all the special things about the toy. What is it made of? How big is it? What can it do? Who could play with it and how much does it cost to buy?

Report

✂

A broken toy

Accidents can happen. Things get broken sometimes, even when we are trying to be very careful. When something like a jar gets broken it can't be fixed, but many toys can be repaired. One of your toys has probably broken at some time.

Try to recall a time when one of your toys was broken. It needs to be a toy that was able to be fixed again. Write down all the things that were needed to fix the toy. Maybe you needed a nail or some thread and a needle. Write down everything that had to be done to fix the toy. Begin with the first thing that was done.

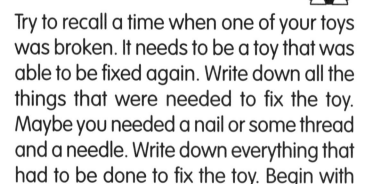

Procedure

49 I was so scared

Most toys we use or play with don't make us scared—but there are some that can. When you were smaller, things probably scared you more than they do now.

Think back to a time when you were scared while on a large moving toy like a swing, a seesaw, a bicycle, or even a merry-go-round.

Write about where you were at the time, what it was that scared you, and what made you feel better.

Reflection

50 My favorite toy

It's amazing how many different toys we get to play with all the time. We can play with toys at home, at school, and when we visit a friend's house. There are even some libraries where we can play with toys.

Draw a picture of your favorite toy. Underneath, write all you can think of about the toy—what it looks like, what you can do with it, and what makes it so special.

Report

51 Police at work

The police have many important jobs to do. They stop people doing the wrong thing, they control traffic, they help at places where there are big crowds of people, and they protect us.

Read and think about this sentence for a little while.

Police officers are our friends.

On your page, write down exactly what you think about this sentence.

Exposition

---

52 What did my teacher do?

Teachers are very busy people. Your teacher does many special things for you and your classmates every day. Even at recess and lunchtime, your teacher probably prepares more activities for you while you are having fun.

Choose one day from the past week. It might be easiest if you choose yesterday. Write about all the things that your teacher did for your class, from when you came into school in the morning until the last bell rang.

Reflection

53 An important job

People have many different jobs. Some people make things and some people work in offices. Others sell things or fix things. All these different sorts of jobs are very important.

Think of a special adult person in your life. What work does that person do? On your paper, write a heading of what the person does. Your heading might say "A Gardener," "A Firefighter," "A Teacher," or "A Shopkeeper." Now write about the job this person does. Try to include as much information as you can about the job.

Report

---

54 What will I be?

When we are young there are many things that we dream of being when we grow up. Sometimes we think we would like to do whatever Mom or Dad does. Sometimes we might pass someone doing a special job and think that's just what we'd like to do.

Think of a job that you would like to do. Write a story pretending that you have the job of your dreams. Include what the job is, where you do it, what happens while you are at work, and how you feel about all that happens while you are doing it.

Narrative

55 Computer teacher

When teachers are explaining how to use something, they need to go through the instructions step by step. If the students don't understand at first, the teacher might need to explain it again.

You are going to be a computer teacher and you are going to explain to a student exactly how he or she can print a story using the computer. All your steps need to be written on your page. Begin by explaining how to turn the computer on.

Procedure

----

56 From the cow to the shop

There are many things which we buy in shops that have come from a long way away. Fruit isn't grown in shops, nor are eggs and bacon, so how do they get there? Of course, there are people who have the special job of driving these goods to the shop.

Let's investigate how we are able to buy milk in shops. Write and explain how the milk gets from the cow to the shop.

Explanation

57

A farmer's magical adventure

A farmer has many different jobs to do on the farm. He or she usually starts work very early in the morning and comes inside late at night.

Write your own story about a farmer who has magical and exciting things happen to him as he goes about doing the different jobs on the farm. Perhaps the animals talk or the machines do silly things. You could begin your story with "Once upon a time."

Narrative

- ✂

58

Work, work, work

There are people working around us all the time. If we stand on a sidewak near some shops we might see a bus driver, a painter, a window cleaner, a taxi driver, and a police officer. If we have the time to watch people doing their jobs, we can learn a lot about the work they do.

Write about a time when you watched someone doing his/her special job. Explain what the job was, where the person was doing it, and what he or she was actually doing.

Reflection

59 Getting paid

Most people get paid for the work they do. Some people get paid a lot of money and some do not get paid much at all. There are some people who don't get paid at all for the work they do. We call them volunteers.

Read the following question:

Should doctors get paid a lot of money?

After you have thought about this question for a little while, write your answer. Try to write several reasons for the answer that you give.

Exposition

---

60 The school custodian

School custodians have a very big job to do. Think of all the classrooms, corridors, and offices that they need to clean. Many of them are also in charge of keeping the outside of the school neat and tidy.

You have probably watched your school custodian do many jobs. At the top of your page, write the heading "School Custodian." Write a report about everything that you think your school custodian does. Maybe your teacher could show it to the custodian.

Report

NOTES

NOTES

NOTES

NOTES